YO

A MISCELLANY

Compiled by Julia Skinner

With particular reference to the work of Maureen Anderson

THE FRANCIS FRITH COLLECTION

www.francisfrith.com

Based on a book first published in the United Kingdom in 2006 by The Francis Frith Collection®

Hardback edition published in 2008 ISBN 978-1-84589-383-5

British Library Cataloguing in Publication Data

Did You Know? York - A Miscellany
Compiled by Julia Skinner
With particular reference to the work of Maureen Anderson

The Francis Frith Collection
Frith's Barn, Teffont,
Salisbury, Wiltshire SP3 5QP
Tel: +44 (0) 1722 716 376
Email: info@francisfrith.co.uk
www.francisfrith.com

Printed and bound in Singapore

Front Cover: **YORK, THE RAILWAY STATION 1909** 61850p

The colour-tinting is for illustrative purposes only, and is not intended to be historically accurate

AS WITH ANY HISTORICAL DATABASE, THE FRANCIS FRITH ARCHIVE IS CONSTANTLY BEING
CORRECTED AND IMPROVED, AND THE PUBLISHERS WOULD WELCOME INFORMATION ON
OMISSIONS OR INACCURACIES

CONTENTS

INTRODUCTION

'The history of York is the history of England.'
George VI.

The ancient walled city of York stands at the heart of the Plain of York. Dominated by its magnificent Minster, York is famous for its chocolate and railways, but this busy modern city stands on historic foundations. In Roman times it was the principal military base in Britain, and it was here in AD306 that Constantine the Great was proclaimed emperor by his army. The Saxons made York the capital of the kingdom of Deira, and in later years, as Jorvik, it was the capital of a Viking kingdom. For many centuries the walled town of York was the second most important city in England, and the walk around the surviving walls is still one of the finest ways to see the city.

Charles I made York his northern headquarters in 1639, and the Parliamentarians laid siege to the city five years later, during the Civil War. After the battle of Marston Moor, fought six miles west of York in 1644, the Royalist garrison surrendered, but only after a promise that the Minster and other city churches would not be desecrated. Today York's marvellous survival as a still mainly medieval city has marked it as one of the great tourist attractions of Britain.

The story of York is full of fascinating characters and events, of which this book can only provide a glimpse. The wealth of preserved history in this amazing city needs days, rather than hours, to explore. Along the snickelways, above the shop fronts, are public house signs, teashop signs, statues, carvings, gargoyles and other reminders of what the buildings were once used for, or who once lived there. A statue of Minerva, the goddess of wisdom, sits with her arm leaning on a pile of books, looking down from the corner of Minster Gates, which was once known as Bookbinder's Alley; in Coney Street,

standing on the top of the clock of St Martin's Church, is 'the little admiral', a naval officer looking through a sextant. Many buildings that have been preserved or painstakingly restored are now open to the public, and at dusk many of them are floodlit. Millions of visitors come from every corner of the world to visit this historic place, and experience its magical atmosphere.

MONK BAR c1955 Y12044

LOCAL WORDS AND PHRASES

'Appen' - perhaps.

'Fendable' - capable.

'It fair trim'd ma' - that suited me perfectly, as of a present.

'Liggin' - lying down.

'Lop' - a flea.

'Menseful' - neat, decent, orderly. **'It will mense it off'** - It will finish something off nicely.

'Putten aboot' - harassed, very busy.

'Sen' - since, ago.

'Side the table' - clear the table.

'Stagnated' or **'fair capp'd'** - greatly surprised.

'Stall'd' - fed up with, wearied or tired of something.

Street names in York are rather confusing: the historic gateways into York are called 'bars'; the term 'gate' in York street names (ie Walmgate, Stonegate) actually means 'street' and derives from the old Viking word 'gata'. A 'yard' is an alley, and a 'court' is a yard.

HAUNTED YORK

It is said that well over 100 ghosts can still be seen or heard in York; the popular Ghost Walks take visitors on a tour of public houses, churches and other buildings as the sad tales behind the hauntings are told.

One story is of the Towpath Ghost, a white headless lady who is said to wander up and down the Ouse towpath looking for the people who robbed and killed her while she was strolling along the riverbank. Her body lay hidden for so long that her head had separated from her body by the time it was found.

One of the most interesting buildings in York is the Treasurer's House. A story tells how a young apprentice plumber once reported that while he was working there in the cellar he heard a trumpet playing, and then saw an army of Roman soldiers marching by, but as if on their knees. When the cellar floor was dug up, the remains of a Roman road were discovered where the soldiers' feet would have been.

Another tale relates how two brothers who rented rooms at St William's College robbed and murdered a cleric. The younger brother hid in a chest with the booty, but was found and hanged after his older brother gave him away. The older brother, although free, was haunted by guilt and died quite young. It is said that his footsteps can still be heard at night pacing the upper floors of the College.

The remaining ruins of St Mary's Abbey, which stand in Museum Gardens, are reputed to be haunted by the ghost of Anne Boleyn, who once stayed there. The terrible cries of dying people who were placed in the abbey courtyard during the Civil War, after an attack by Parliamentarian forces, are also said to have been heard there.

Unsurprisingly considering its gruesome history (see page 21), there are frequent stories of ghosts frequenting Micklegate Bar, including a mysterious gentleman dressed in black.

Holy Trinity Church at Micklegate is famously haunted by three ghosts, a mother and her child and another woman, possibly a nursemaid.

The decapitated ghost of Thomas Percy, 7th Earl of Northumberland, executed at York in 1572, is said to roam near Holy Trinity Church, Goodramgate, searching for his head.

YORK MISCELLANY

Monk Bar, seen in photograph Y12019, opposite, is one of the finest gates in the city walls. With four storeys, and standing at 63ft high, it is the tallest of the four main bars, and also the most fortified - it was a self-contained fortress, and still has a working portcullis. As with all the bars, the rooms of Monk Bar have had many different uses, including being used as a prison in the 16th century. The statues on the parapet are holding rocks and boulders, and stand ready to throw them at any invader.

York began in AD71 as a Roman camp, which was home to some 6,000 soldiers. Near the soldiers' encampment a civilian town grew up, which was peopled by traders and their families who supplied the soldiers with food, clothing and suchlike. One Roman building that still stands is the Multiangular Tower (see photograph 18485, page 8). A Roman column which was found during excavations to the Minster in 1969, lying where it had fallen, was erected in the Minster Yard in 1971 by the York Civic Trust.

York takes its name from the Latinised Celtic 'Eboracum', meaning either 'the estate of Eburos' or possibly 'the place of yew trees', which was used in Roman times. The Anglo-Saxons added 'wic' to create 'Eoforwic', which was rendered as 'Jorvik' by the Vikings during their period of occupation, and the name eventually became York.

MONK BAR c1950 Y12019

THE MULTIANGULAR TOWER c1885 18485

The lower part of the strange structure known as the Multiangular Tower is Roman (see photograph 18485, above); it was the west corner of the Roman fort. The upper part is 14th-century. Inside, there is a small ruined tower. When this stretch of the wall was excavated, the archaeologists found that the ramparts dated from Roman, Saxon, Viking, Norman and medieval times, and that the earth bank grew with each occupation.

A public house called the Roman Bath Inn in St Sampson's Square has a floor made up of panels of glass where one can look onto the remains of a Roman bath-house that was excavated there in 1930.

Bootham Bar was the main exit from the medieval walled city of York (see photograph 63585, below). It was built on the site of the Roman gate, the 'Porta Principalis', and probably much of the stone was reused. Bootham Bar was one of four major 'bars' in the city; the portcullis and winding gear are still there. In 1832, plans to demolish the whole structure were halted after a public outcry. The name Bootham derives from 'Butham', meaning 'at the booths', and probably referred to market stalls that were set up nearby.

BOOTHAM BAR 1911 63585

LENDAL BRIDGE 1909 61702

Lendal Bridge, seen in this photograph, was made of cast-iron and was opened in 1863. It improved the city by giving direct access to the original railway station, which was situated within the city walls.

WALMGATE BAR c1885 18448

Walmgate Bar (see photograph 18448, above) was the principal entrance to York from the south-east; travellers would then cross the city and leave it via the Bootham Bar. The Barbican, or outer gateway, was added in the 13th century, and Walmgate Bar is the only one of the four 'bars' that has retained its barbican. Accommodation in the shape of a timber-framed house on the inner side of the bar was added in the 16th century, and it was lived in until 1960; John Browne, historian and artist of the Minster, was born in the house in 1793. During the 1644 siege of York during the Civil War, Walmgate Bar came under heavy attack by cannons and mines, and there was also an attempt to undermine it with gunpowder; the mine caused the ground to subside over time, which is probably the cause of the sagging in the side walls that is still visible.

Bootham Bar is the oldest of York's gates through the medieval walls. In the Middle Ages, guards were posted there to keep watch and to guide people from the nearby Forest of Galtres so as to protect them from the packs of wolves that roamed the area.

The awe-inspiring and formidable walls and gate of York's castle seen in photograph 18492, below, were knocked down in 1934. At that time there were no conservation laws, and anything that was in the way of progress was destroyed. The walls once surrounded both the castle and Clifford's Tower. The site of the old gate is now a car park.

THE CASTLE GATE c1885 18492

In AD306, Constantine I was hailed as the Roman emperor by his troops in York, the only Roman emperor to be proclaimed in Britain. He has become known as Constantine the Great because he was the emperor who was responsible for the official acceptance of Christianity in the Roman empire in AD313. The pagan Constantine's acceptance of Christianity came about when, on the eve of an important battle in northern Italy at Milvian Bridge, he had a dream in which he saw the Chi-Rho sign (the first two letters of Christ's name in Greek), and heard a voice saying: 'In this sign conquer'. He changed the Roman Labarum, a banner with a wreath-like circle, to include the Chi-Rho sign. He won the battle, and thereafter Christianity was permitted throughout the Roman empire. It is interesting that Constantine did not become converted himself until he was on his deathbed in AD330 - he clearly wished to hedge his bets! A modern statue of Constantine I can be seen outside the Minster, but it is interesting to compare this with a marble head of the emperor which was sculpted in Roman times, which was found in Stonegate and can be seen in the Yorkshire Museum in Museum Street.

Photograph 6619, opposite, shows the ruins of St Mary's Abbey in Museum Gardens. Founded c1055, this was originally a Benedictine abbey dedicated to St Olave, but in 1088 the monastery was re-sited and became known as St Mary's Abbey, eventually becoming one of the largest and wealthiest Benedictine houses in the north of England. Only a few fragments of the abbey church survive, but the remains of the north aisle walls show some of the fine arcading that once decorated the internal walls of the church. However, the Norman gatehouse, the old Abbot's House, and the 14th-century timber-framed guesthouse (the Hospitium - see page 16) of the abbey still remain. The abbey was dissolved in 1539.

ST MARY'S ABBEY c1873 6619

THE HOSPITIUM c1885 18483

The Hospitium, situated in what is now the Museum Gardens
(see photograph 18483, above), was the guest house for St
Mary's Abbey The ground floor was built in the early 14th
century, while the timber-framed first floor was added in 1420.
A new roof was built in the 1930s.

After the Norman Conquest, William I erected two motte and bailey
castles at York, one on each side of the River Ouse. Both the castles
were sacked in 1069, when the people of York rose up against
Norman rule. The castle on the west bank of the river was never
rebuilt, but its earthworks can still be seen around Baile Hill. Clifford's
Tower stands on the mound of the Norman castle on the east bank of
the Ouse.

The coming of the railways put York firmly on the tourist map; York's first railway station was built in 1839. Though the lines were owned by the North Eastern, no less than five other companies had running powers into the city.

The magnificent stained-glass window above the high altar in York Minster, seen in photograph 70640, below, was made in the 13th century and is larger than a tennis court. Re-leading of the window was begun when it was removed from the Minster for safety during the Second World War; the mammoth task took ten years to complete.

THE MINSTER, THE CHOIR EAST 1921 70640

17

The Barracks on Fulford Road, shown in the photograph below, were built around 1795 for the 14th Regimental District and the West Yorkshire Regiment as part of William Pitt's defence programme. They became the Imphal Barracks in 1951, named

after the West Yorkshire Regiment's defence of the Imphal plains in India in 1944. The large keep seen in the photograph is still in use. A 25-pounder gun and a Saladin armoured car are preserved on the site.

THE INFANTRY BARRACKS, THE ARMOURY 1886 18710

MICKLEGATE BAR c1885 18440

Micklegate Bar (photograph 18440, opposite) was the gateway that led to the road to London. In the 10th century, when permission was granted for a house to be built over the bar, the yearly rent charged was sixpence. Eventually Micklegate Bar commanded the highest rent of the four bars at just over thirteen shillings. The walls of the passage are built with Roman stone, including used coffins. Micklegate Bar has a gruesome place in York's history, for it was here that the heads of executed traitors and conspirators were often displayed on pikes. The head of Richard, Duke of York was put on display following the Battle of Wakefield in 1460. The last heads to be displayed here were those of William Connolly and James Mayne, executed for their part in the Jacobite Rebellion of 1745-46. The government called a halt to the practice in 1754 after the heads of Connolly and Mayne were stolen by a Jacobite tailor. He was caught and fined £5, and sentenced to two years in jail.

Clifford's Tower was probably named after Roger de Clifford, whose body was hung from the tower in chains in 1322 after he rebelled against Edward II (see photograph Y12018 on page 33). It was twice built in timber, and then rebuilt in stone. Because of the moat surrounding the tower there were problems with subsidence; eventually it cracked in two places from top to bottom. In the 16th century Robert Redhead, a gaoler, wanted to demolish the tower, but the people of York and the Corporation decided it should be kept as a treasure second only to the Minster. For over 100 years, from about 1825, the tower was included in the grounds of York's prison, and a high wall surrounded both the tower and the prison buildings, with no access to the public. The tower is now cared for by English Heritage.

The medieval church of Holy Trinity at Goodramgate (see photograph 61857, opposite) is the second oldest in York, and is looked after by the Churches Conservation Trust. It is adorned with beautiful 15th-century stained-glass, donated by the Reverend John Walker, rector of the church in the early 1470s.

When the mission of St Augustine came from Rome to convert Anglo-Saxon England to Christianity in AD597, instructions were given by Pope Gregory that the new English Church was to be governed from the former Roman capitals of London and York. The Archbishopric of London never materialised, but that of York was successfully established by St Paulinus. During the Anglo-Saxon period York became a centre of learning, something like an equivalent of a university. One of the most famous scholars who was educated there was Alcuin of York, who later became a monk and a teacher there himself. Alcuin went on to become one of the chief advisors on religious and educational matters to King Charles the Great of France (AD768-814), better known to history as Charlemagne.

The present Minster was not the first place of worship to be built on the site. It stands on land previously occupied by the Roman praetorium, and then by various churches; the earliest of these was a small wattle oratory constructed for the baptism of Edwin, King of Northumbria, in AD627. Some of these early churches were destroyed by fires, the worst of which was in 1137, which not only raged through the church but also destroyed a large part of the town, including St Mary's Abbey and a number of other churches.

HOLY TRINITY CHURCH, GOODRAMGATE 1909 61857

THE MINSTER 1908 59785

Begun during the reign of King John and finally completed in 1472, York Minster is one of the largest cathedrals of England, and the western towers are 196ft high. Between 1829 and 1984 there were three fires at the Minster; the first was caused deliberately, the second by a careless workman, and the third by lightning. All three caused damage and loss, and much restoration work has had to be carried out.

A story is told - which may or may not be true - that in 1154 thousands of people lined the old bridge over the River Ouse to welcome the arrival of Archbishop William Fitzherbert, later to become St William of York. The weight of the crowds caused the bridge to collapse, but no one was killed. Because there was no loss of life, the event was proclaimed a miracle.

The Gee Monument in the Minster, shown in photograph 61713, below, commemorates Sir William Gee, secretary to James I and a member of his privy council. It was erected by his widow, Mary, after his death in 1611. It shows Sir William, his two wives and five children at prayer.

THE MINSTER, THE GEE MONUMENT 1909 61713

The new station seen in photograph 61849 (below) was built to replace the original station built in 1839, and construction took place between 1873 and 1877 on the site of a Roman cemetery. When it was completed it was said to be the largest station in the

THE RAILWAY STATION AND THE HOTEL 1909 61849

world. When this second station was constructed, new openings had to be made in the city walls to give better access; much of the city street plan was also changed - for example, Thieves Lane became the much more salubrious Station Road.

ST WILLIAM'S COLLEGE 1920 69602

THE MANSION HOUSE c1955 Y12048

St William's College (see photograph 69602, opposite) was first built for the Minster's chantry priests, in about 1465. The building was named after Archbishop William Fitzherbert, who was the great-grandson of William the Conqueror. When Charles I moved his court to York during the Civil War, the royal printing press was housed here.

All Saints' Church in North Street is famous for two interesting stained-glass windows. The 'Prykke of Conscience' window, which was designed in the 15th century, shows that not all medieval stained-glass illustrated biblical scenes: intended as a warning of what was to come, it depicts the 'Last 15 Days of the World' in 15 panels, with accompanying text, such as 'the 11th day when men emerge from their shelters and pray for help', and 'the 14th day when death comes to claim all mortals'. The scenes are based on the 'Prykke of Conscience', which was written by the English mystic Richard Rolle in the Northumbrian dialect in 1325. The 'Corporal Acts of Mercy' window shows the six acts of mercy that can be given to the living (the seventh, burying the dead, is not depicted); these are: feeding the hungry, giving drink to the thirsty, offering hospitality to strangers, clothing the naked, visiting the sick and comforting those in prison. It is thought that the window may have been given as a memorial to a merchant of York called Nicholas Blackburn, who was also a mayor of the city, and that Nicholas may be the bearded man performing the acts of mercy in each panel.

The Mansion House in St Helen's Square (see photograph Y12048, opposite) was built c1775 as the Lord Mayor's residence. It is now one of the three oldest surviving buildings of its kind in England.

In the 9th century the Vikings took over York, calling it 'Jorvik'; the last Viking king of Jorvik was the delightfully-named Eric Bloodaxe, who died in AD954. Some of the city's place names, such as Micklegate and Goodramgate, are inheritances from this time, although the Vikings were only here for less than a century. Although there is little evidence of the Viking period above ground, excavations have turned up many well-preserved artefacts. The Jorvik Viking Centre, a huge tourist attraction which brings large numbers of visitors to York each year, is built upon the site of an excavated Viking settlement, and the artefacts found here can be seen in the museum. Even the Viking rubbish dumps were a treasure trove to the archaeologists: shoes, utensils and items of discarded clothing all serve to illuminate the Viking way of life.

York Minster boasts wonderful Gothic architecture, woodwork and stonework, and particularly stained-glass, 128 windows in all, spanning 800 years of glass painting. The second window on the left, as the visitor enters through the nave's west door, has what is said to be the oldest glass in England, dating from about 1150. More than half of England's surviving medieval stained-glass is contained in the Minster, which is particularly famous for its magnificent Rose Window. Also noteworthy is the beautiful west window with its heart-shaped tracery, which is known as 'the Heart of Yorkshire'.

For centuries the River Ouse was used to transport people and goods in and out of the city. In the mid 1830s there was even a steamer service linking York with London. The journey took over 30 hours, and at that time was considered an acceptable alternative to being shaken and bounced along the Great North Road in a mail-coach.

STONEGATE 1886 18449

THE SHAMBLES 1909 61722

A 16th-century York woman, Margaret Clitheroe, was canonised by Pope Paul VI in 1970. Margaret was married to a butcher and lived in the Shambles. She was arrested for harbouring Roman Catholic priests, and was tried at what was then the Common Hall (now the Guildhall). She refused to plead, was found guilty and was sentenced to death in 1586 by the barbaric method of 'pressing', or being crushed to death beneath a board. A house in the Shambles is now set aside as a shrine to her.

York was afflicted by a cholera epidemic in 1832, and many of the victims laid to rest in a burial ground outside the city walls along the section near the railway station and the Station Hotel.

The coming of the railway to York had a huge impact on the economy of the city, and brought prosperity to many. George Hudson, dubbed 'the Railway King', was instrumental in the development of the railway and its related buildings. Hudson was three times Lord Mayor, but eventually crooked wheeling and dealing with funds brought about his downfall. For over a century his name was shunned in York, and George Hudson Street was renamed Railway Street. However, in recent years his contribution to the city has been recognised; a street and a building have been named after him, and Railway Street became George Hudson Street again in 1971.

CLIFFORD'S TOWER c1950 Y12018

All Saints' Church, Pavement, has an interesting lantern tower from which in ancient times a lantern was hung to help guide travellers through the Forest of Galtres. The church is said to be the last

ST MARY'S TOWER c1885 18455

resting place of 39 Lord Mayors of York. It is the Guild Church of York, and contains a 17th-century pulpit from which John Wesley preached.

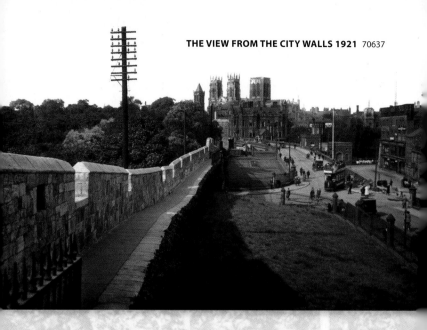

In July 1984 York Minster was struck by lightning, which set the south transept ablaze. Damage was severe, and the great Rose Window suffered thousands of cracks. The strike was seen by some as a sign that the Almighty was displeased with the views of the recently enthroned Bishop of Durham's questioning of the virgin birth and resurrection.

Although the chimneystacks and the large dull grey buildings relating to heavy industry never made a serious impact on York, the sweet industry made its mark. The origins of Rowntree Mackintosh's and Terry's chocolate empires began in retail businesses in York in the 18th century. The businesses developed into large-scale confectionery manufacture; in the late 1930s they were employing over 12,000 people. Both these firms are still major players in the confectionery and food industry today.

The Castle Museum occupies two classical-style 18th-century buildings originally built as the prisons for debtors and for women. It is one of the leading folk museums in the country, where life from Tudor to Victorian times is shown by a series of reconstructed cobbled streets flanked by picturesque buildings.

Lendal Tower was once linked by a chain to Barker's Tower on the opposite side of the river to stop craft entering the city without paying a tax. From the 17th century the tower was a pumping house for York's water supply - the wheel was turned by horses.

LENDAL TOWER c1885 18456

THE RAILWAY STATION 1909 61850

THE OUSE BRIDGE 1885 18463

The Assize Court at York Castle was built in the 1770s. The area is known as 'The Eye of Yorkshire', or 'The Eye of the Ridings'. Many notorious criminals were tried at York, including the legendary highwayman Dick Turpin in 1739. When Turpin was apprehended he was using the name of Palmer, and he was tried for horse stealing, although the full catalogue of his crimes included robbery and murder. It was not until after he was arrested that his true identity was discovered. He spent his final days in the condemned cell of York's prison, and was hanged at the gallows at Tyburn, on the Tadcaster Road. Turpin's grave may be seen in St George's churchyard. Dick Turpin is famous in folklore for a legendary ride on his horse Black Bess from London to York, but this ride was actually done 60 years earlier by another highwayman, William Nevison, who was also hanged at York, in 1684.

The term 'bygones' was coined by a young doctor from near Pickering, John Kirk, in the early part of the 20th century. He felt that many everyday items were disappearing, often being thrown away because of more modern replacements, so he started a collection of discarded country objects and included everything from furniture to kitchen utensils. Wishing his collection to be displayed, he approached many towns and cities in the area, but no one was interested until Alderman J Morrell in York backed his idea. The old female prison at York was turned into the Kirk Museum. It became an instant success and has remained a huge attraction in York, now incorporated into the Castle Museum.

York had a long wait for a university, but once plans were approved, work went ahead quickly. Some older historical buildings were incorporated into the structure of the plans, and the first two colleges were opened in the 1960s, with others following over the next few years. In 2003, the Sunday Times named the University of York as its 'University of the Year'.

Tradition still plays a key role in York. At Christmas the high altar in the Minster has mistletoe placed upon it as decoration; the plant is said to have magical properties and its associations are pagan, so it is unknown how this practice came to be. Displays of sword dancing are held in St Sampson's Square on Plough Monday (the first Monday after 6 January); again, the origins of this custom are unknown - the dancing was once performed by farm labourers. The famous Mystery Plays are still performed in the Minster Yard, usually by amateur groups; all the plays tell biblical stories, which in medieval times were performed by members of the local craft guilds - the word 'mystery' derives from the 'mastery' of the craftsmen.

An exhibition of fine art was held in the grounds of Bootham Park Hospital in 1866. It attracted thousands of people, so it was decided that a permanent building for further exhibitions should be erected. This building, in what became known as Exhibition Square, opened in 1879; it is now the York Art Gallery, and has recently undergone a major refurbishment programme. Amongst its collection is work by Monet, Rembrandt, Lowry, Reynolds and Titian. Between the arches of the entrance to the gallery are roundels depicting four famous artistic men of York: John Carr (architect), John Camidge (musician), John Flaxman (sculptor), and William Etty (painter).

SPORTING YORK

York has been associated with horse racing ever since the early days of the sport's popularity. Some of the early meetings were timed to coincide with the York assizes, and the Knavesmire was the location for both horse racing and public executions from 1731. The introduction of two major races in the 1840s, the Ebor Handicap and the Gimcrack Stakes, was the basis for the course's later success.

Although never a major force in the game, there has been a professional Rugby League club in York since as far back as 1901, the club being based at Clarence Street until 1989. The club's greatest achievements came between the two World Wars, winning the prestigious Yorkshire Cup on three occasions. Since then, successes have been rare. In recent years the club went bankrupt and was re-founded as York City Knights. However, the club won National League Two in 2005, bringing a return to the second tier of English Rugby League.

York's most famous footballing personality is Steve McClaren. He was born in Fulford in 1961, and played school football in the city. After a ten year playing career in the lower leagues, he went into management and rose quickly through the coaching ranks at Manchester United and Middlesbrough. He received the highest honour of his profession when he was appointed England manager in 2006.

York City FC was founded in 1922. After achieving league status the club has spent most of its history in the lower leagues, although it did spend two years in Division Two in the mid 1970s. The club's finest run was in 1954, reaching the FA Cup semi final. The Cup run included a win against Blackpool, which had the great Stanley Matthews in its side, and in the semi final York City took Newcastle United to a replay. York City also achieved an extraordinary victory during the 1994/95 season, in the League Cup, winning 3-0 away to Manchester United.

QUIZ QUESTIONS

Answers on page 48.

1. How did Stonegate get its name?

2. Which trade was associated with the Shambles in medieval times?

3. What is the connection between York and Bonfire Night?

4. Where and what is 'The Monkey's Funeral'?

5. Since medieval times, the title of Duke of York has traditionally been given to the second son of the sovereign. How many Dukes of York have eventually been crowned king?

6. Who do the statues on the top of Bootham Bar represent?

7. Lund's Court which links Swinegate with Low Petergate was formerly known as Mad Alice Lane - who was Mad Alice, and what happened to her?

8. Where can you see a wooden mouse on a door?

9. Why is there a figure of a red devil by the entrance to Coffee Yard, above the shop front of No 33 Stonegate?

10. Who is represented by the statue in Exhibition Square, in front of York Art Gallery, and what is he famous for?

THE MINSTER AND ST WILLIAM'S COLLEGE
1908 59795

RECIPE

TOM TROTT TOFFEE

This treacle toffee is traditionally eaten in Yorkshire on Bonfire Night, 5 November, and is particularly appropriate for York - see quiz question 3!

Ingredients

450g/1lb soft brown sugar	2 teaspoonfuls of vinegar
5 tablespoonfuls of water	25g/1oz butter
	150ml/¼ pint black treacle

Put the sugar into a saucepan with the water and vinegar and when dissolved add the butter and the treacle. Heat gently until the butter and treacle melt. Raise the heat and boil for 12-15 minutes. The temperature can be checked with a sugar thermometer, and should reach around 140 degrees C/ 280 degrees F.

Pour the treacle into an oiled tin and leave until partially set. Score the toffee with a knife into bars or squares, and when cold break up and store in an airtight tin.

THE MARKET 1908 59799

GALA

LOW PETERGATE c1960 Y12060

RECIPE

YORKSHIRE FAT RASCALS

Ingredients

450g/1lb plain flour
225g/8oz butter
25g/1oz light soft brown
sugar

Pinch of salt
115g/4oz currants
A small quantity of milk and
water mixed

Rub the butter into the flour. Add the sugar, salt and currants and mix to a firm dough with a little water and milk. Roll out to about 1cm (½ inch) thick, and cut into 6cm (2½ inch) rounds. Dust with a little caster sugar and bake at 180 degrees C/350 degrees F/Gas Mark 4 for about 20 minutes.

QUIZ ANSWERS

1. Stonegate probably means that the street was paved with stone; the name derives from Viking times, and may show that the street still retained its Roman paving stones at that date, although another theory suggests that the street got its name because the stone used in the construction of York Minster was carried along this route.

2. The word 'shambles' comes from the Old English 'shamel', which means 'a bench or stall', and in medieval times this was the area of the town where the butchers prepared and sold meat from such 'shambles'. The wide shelves for displaying meat can be seen at the front of the shops in photograph 61722 (on page 32), and these and the hooks overhead indicate that even in the early years of the 20th century this was still the traditional part of the city for butchers' shops. The narrowness of the street kept the shops cool in the days before refrigeration, and prevented direct sunlight from reaching the meat.

3. Guy Fawkes, who was born in York in 1570. He was recruited by the Gunpowder Plotters because of his expertise with gunpowder, gained during his military career. Guy Fawkes was caught in the cellars of the House of Lords in 1605, apparently about to blow up James I and his parliament with 36 barrels of powder, and was executed along with the other conspirators. The event is commemorated on Bonfire Night, 5 November.

4. One panel of a medieval window in York Minster shows that the painter had a sense of humour: it depicts what is known as 'The Monkey's Funeral'. Nine monkeys are pictured. The deceased is carried shoulder-high by four pall-bearers, while a bellringer leads the procession with a cross-bearer behind. The bereaved young monkey is in the centre foreground, being comforted by a friend. Last but not least, one monkey is sampling the wine at the funeral feast.

5. Six Dukes of York have become reigning monarchs: Edward IV, Henry VIII, Charles I, James II, George V and George VI.

6. The statues can be seen in photograph 63585 on page 9. They were carved in 1894 by George Milburn to replace the older, worn statues, and represent Nicholas Langton (a Lord Mayor), a mason holding a model of Bootham Bar and a medieval knight. The coats of arms are the royal arms of the House of Stuart and the arms of the city of York; these were renewed in 1969.

7. Mad Alice was Alice Smith, who lived in the lane until she was arrested and tried for poisoning her husband. She pleaded insanity in her defence, but to no avail, and was hanged in 1825.

8. The central doors of St William's College were made by the famous wood carver, Robert Thompson of Kilburn, 'the Mouseman'. His signature, a mouse, is carved on the right-hand door. The College is now open to the public as a restaurant and exhibition hall.

9. This shows that the building was a printer's shop in earlier times. The boys who fetched and carried the hot metal type for printers were known as 'printers' devils'. The first known press was in Stonegate in 1509, and the first newspaper in York was printed in this area of the city in 1719.

10. The statue represents the artist William Etty, born in York in 1787. He attended the Royal Academy School from 1806, and was elected to membership of the Royal Academy in 1825. He travelled widely in Italy, and was particularly inspired by the works of Titian, Veronese and Rubens. He is famous for being the first British painter before the 20th century to specialise in painting female nudes; this brought him some degree of public censure, but he justified his interest with the words 'as all human beauty is concentrated in woman I will dedicate myself to paint her.'

CONEY STREET 1909 61723

CENTRAL GARAGE

BARGES ON THE OUSE 1886 18494

FRANCIS FRITH

PIONEER VICTORIAN PHOTOGRAPHER

Francis Frith, founder of the world-famous photographic archive, was a complex and multi-talented man. A devout Quaker and a highly successful Victorian businessman, he was philosophical by nature and pioneering in outlook. By 1855 he had already established a wholesale grocery business in Liverpool, and sold it for the astonishing sum of £200,000, which is the equivalent today of over £15,000,000. Now in his thirties, and captivated by the new science of photography, Frith set out on a series of pioneering journeys up the Nile and to the Near East.

INTRIGUE AND EXPLORATION

He was the first photographer to venture beyond the sixth cataract of the Nile. Africa was still the mysterious 'Dark Continent', and Stanley and Livingstone's historic meeting was a decade into the future. The conditions for picture taking confound belief. He laboured for hours in his wicker dark-room in the sweltering heat of the desert, while the volatile chemicals fizzed dangerously in their trays. Back in London he exhibited his photographs and was 'rapturously cheered' by members of the Royal Society. His reputation as a photographer was made overnight.

VENTURE OF A LIFE-TIME

By the 1870s the railways had threaded their way across the country, and Bank Holidays and half-day Saturdays had been made obligatory by Act of Parliament. All of a sudden the working man and his family were able to enjoy days out, take holidays, and see a little more of the world.

With typical business acumen, Francis Frith foresaw that these new tourists would enjoy having souvenirs to commemorate their days out. For the next thirty years he travelled the country by train and by pony and trap, producing fine photographs of seaside resorts and beauty spots that were keenly bought by millions of Victorians. These prints were painstakingly pasted into family albums and pored over during the dark nights of winter, rekindling precious memories of summer excursions. Frith's studio was soon supplying retail shops all over the country, and by 1890 F Frith & Co had become the greatest specialist photographic publishing company in the world, with over 2,000 sales outlets, and pioneered the picture postcard.

FRANCIS FRITH'S LEGACY

Francis Frith had died in 1898 at his villa in Cannes, his great project still growing. By 1970 the archive he created contained over a third of a million pictures showing 7,000 British towns and villages.

Frith's legacy to us today is of immense significance and value, for the magnificent archive of evocative photographs he created provides a unique record of change in the cities, towns and villages throughout Britain over a century and more. Frith and his fellow studio photographers revisited locations many times down the years to update their views, compiling for us an enthralling and colourful pageant of British life and character.

We are fortunate that Frith was dedicated to recording the minutiae of everyday life. For it is this sheer wealth of visual data, the painstaking chronicle of changes in dress, transport, street layouts, buildings, housing and landscape that captivates us so much today, offering us a powerful link with the past and with the lives of our ancestors.

Computers have now made it possible for Frith's many thousands of images to be accessed almost instantly. The archive offers every one of us an opportunity to examine the places where we and our families have lived and worked down the years. Its images, depicting our shared past, are now bringing pleasure and enlightenment to millions around the world a century and more after his death.

For further information visit: www.francisfrith.com

INTERIOR DECORATION

Frith's photographs can be seen framed and as giant wall murals in thousands of pubs, restaurants, hotels, banks, retail stores and other public buildings throughout Britain. These provide interesting and attractive décor, generating strong local interest and acting as a powerful reminder of gentler days in our increasingly busy and frenetic world.

FRITH PRODUCTS

All Frith photographs are available as prints and posters in a variety of different sizes and styles. In the UK we also offer a range of other gift and stationery products illustrated with Frith photographs, although many of these are not available for delivery outside the UK – see our web site for more information on the products available for delivery in your country.

THE INTERNET

Over 100,000 photographs of Britain can be viewed and purchased on the Frith web site. The web site also includes memories and reminiscences contributed by our customers, who have personal knowledge of localities and of the people and properties depicted in Frith photographs. If you wish to learn more about a specific town or village you may find these reminiscences fascinating to browse. Why not add your own comments if you think they would be of interest to others? See **www.francisfrith.com**

PLEASE HELP US BRING FRITH'S PHOTOGRAPHS TO LIFE

Our authors do their best to recount the history of the places they write about. They give insights into how particular towns and villages developed, they describe the architecture of streets and buildings, and they discuss the lives of famous people who lived there. But however knowledgeable our authors are, the story they tell is necessarily incomplete.

Frith's photographs are so much more than plain historical documents. They are living proofs of the flow of human life down the generations. They show real people at real moments in history; and each of those people is the son or daughter of someone, the brother or sister, aunt or uncle, grandfather or grandmother of someone else. All of them lived, worked and played in the streets depicted in Frith's photographs.

We would be grateful if you would give us your insights into the places shown in our photographs: the streets and buildings, the shops, businesses and industries. Post your memories of life in those streets on the Frith website: what it was like growing up there, who ran the local shop and what shopping was like years ago; if your workplace is shown tell us about your working day and what the building is used for now. Read other visitors' memories and reconnect with your shared local history and heritage. With your help more and more Frith photographs can be brought to life, and vital memories preserved for posterity, and for the benefit of historians in the future.

Wherever possible, we will try to include some of your comments in future editions of our books. Moreover, if you spot errors in dates, titles or other facts, please let us know, because our archive records are not always completely accurate—they rely on 140 years of human endeavour and hand-compiled records. You can email us using the contact form on the website.

Thank you!

For further information, trade, or author enquiries please contact us at the address below:

The Francis Frith Collection, Frith's Barn, Teffont, Salisbury, Wiltshire, England SP3 5QP.
Tel: +44 (0)1722 716 376 Fax: +44 (0)1722 716 881
e-mail: sales@francisfrith.co.uk **www.francisfrith.com**